A Visit to
FRANCE

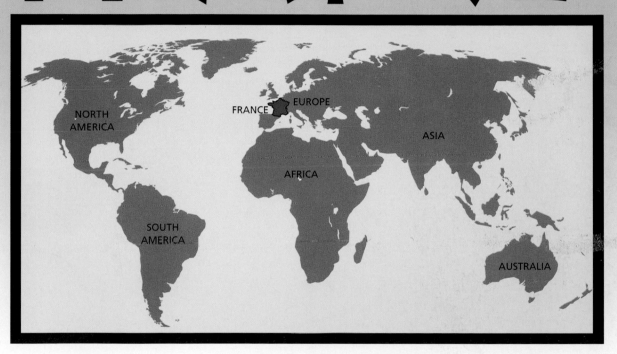

NORTH
AMERICA

FRANCE EUROPE

ASIA

AFRICA

SOUTH
AMERICA

AUSTRALIA

Rob Alcraft

Heinemann
LIBRARY

First published in Great Britain by Heinemann Library,
Halley Court, Jordan Hill, Oxford OX2 8EJ
a division of Reed Educational and Professional Publishing Ltd.

Heinemann is a registered trademark of Reed Educational & Professional Publishing Ltd.

OXFORD MELBOURNE AUCKLAND
JOHANNESBURG BLANTYRE GABORONE
IBADAN PORTSMOUTH (NH) USA CHICAGO

Designed by AMR
Illustrations by Art Construction
Printed in Hong Kong/China

04 03 02 01 00
10 9 8 7 6 5 4 3 2 1

ISBN 0 431 08337 1

This title is also available in a hardback library edition (ISBN 0 431 08332 0).

British Library Cataloguing in Publication Data

Alcraft, Rob 1966 –
  A visit to France
  1.France – Juvenile literature
  I.Title II.France
  944

Acknowledgements
The Publishers would like to thank the following for permission to reproduce photographs:
Bridgeman Art Library, p. 28; Image Bank, p.18; J Allan Cash, pp. 17, 25; Rex Features, (Sipa Press), p. 29; Robert Harding Picture Library, p. 9; (Robert Francis) p. 5; (Adam Woolfitt) p. 6; (Nik Wheeler) p. 15; (K Gillham) p. 21; (Tomlinson) p. 26; Telegraph Colour Library (C B Knight) p. 16; (Richard Cooke) p. 19; (Kathy Collins) p. 27; Trevor Clifford, pp. 13, 17; Trip, (D Hastilow) p. 7; (A Tovy) p. 8; (J Braund) p. 10; (P Rauter) p. 11; (A M Bazalik) p. 12; (Ask Images) p. 22; (S Grant) p. 20; (R Cracknell) p. 23; (B Gadsby) p. 24.

Cover photograph reproduced with permission of Eye Ubiquitous (H. Hedworth)

Every effort has been made to contact copyright holders of any material reproduced in this book. Any omissions will be rectified in subsequent printings if notice is given to the Publisher.

Any words appearing in bold, **like this**, are explained in the Glossary.

Contents

France

Key
- Land above 1000m
- Land above 500m
- Land above 200m
- Land above 0m/sea level
- ● Capital
- ⩕ Eiffel Tower
- ⋔⋔⋔ Pont du Gard
- ·–··– Boundary

ENGLAND
ENGLISH CHANNEL
BELGIUM
GERMANY
R. Somme
Paris
R. Seine
R. Loire
FRANCE
SWITZERLAND
North
R. Dordogne
R. Rhône
A L P S
ITALY
Cannes
Pyrénées
SPAIN
MEDITERRANEAN SEA

France is a big country. It is in Europe.

A quarter of France is forest. There are lakes and rivers. There are gentle valleys where grapes grow.

Land

In the north of France there are green fields and **meadows**. The weather is cool, and it often rains. Farmers grow **wheat** and keep cows.

In the south of France there are high
mountains, and the Mediterranean Sea.
Up in the mountains it is cool and wet.
By the sea it is sunny and dry.

Landmarks

This is the Eiffel Tower, in the middle of Paris. Paris is France's **capital** city. It is the biggest city in France.

This is a bridge, called the Pont du Gard.
It was built to carry water to an ancient
city. It is 2000 years old.

Homes

In cities like Paris most people live in flats. Most windows have wooden **shutters** to keep the rooms cool in summer.

Many smaller towns and villages in France are very old. There are shady squares and narrow streets with old houses built from stone.

Food

Each **region** of France makes its own kinds of cheese, sausage and wine. A good snack is local cheese, with a long stick of French bread, which is very fresh and crisp.

In France families sit together to eat.
This family is enjoying a simple
breakfast of coffee, bread and jam.

13

Clothes

Many young French people wear jeans, training shoes and colourful T-shirts, jumpers and coats. Some older people still wear a special French hat called a béret.

For festivals and parties people still dress up in old French costumes. Women wear white blouses, **bonnets**, and long black skirts with colourful patterns.

Work

France is famous for its **fashion**.
Some people have jobs in the fashion
industry, making and selling clothes.

In the country many farmers grow olive trees. The olives can be eaten or made into oil for cooking.

Transport

France has very fast **motorways**, which you have to pay to use. The busiest one runs in a big loop round Paris.

French trains are comfortable and very fast. They can go at 300kph. There are airports in most cities too. The **canals** and rivers are busy with **barges**.

Language

In France people speak French. French sounds very different from English, but it is written in the same way, from left to right. It uses the same alphabet too.

Different **regions** of France have their own **dialects**. French is also spoken in many parts of the world.

School

In most of France there is school six days a week. Wednesday afternoons are free. French children study maths, geography, and learn English.

Some French schools have special
holidays. The whole class will go off
and have lessons by the beach for a
week. Or in the winter the class will go
and learn how to ski.

Free time

Young people play sports like football in parks and squares. Sometimes they watch TV or visit friends. In the summer they might swim at the beach or in the river.

On warm summer evenings many French people like to sit in pavement cafés, and watch the world go by. Some people play a game called **pétanque** in market squares.

Celebrations

One of the biggest celebrations in France is called Mardi Gras. Everyone has a big party, and there are fireworks and **parades** along city streets.

Many French towns and villages have their own special celebration. It might be on a Saint's Day, or to celebrate the **harvest**. Some are in honour of the local cheese, or that year's new wine.

The Arts

There have been many very famous French painters. This is a painting by Renoir. He wanted his paintings to show how beautiful and colourful the world is.

Making films is important in France.
In May there is a special film festival at a
town called Cannes. People come from all
over the world to see the new films.

Factfile

Name	The French Republic
Capital	France's **capital** city is called Paris.
Language	French
Population	There are 58 million people living in France.
Money	French money is called the franc.
Religion	Most French people are Christians.
Products	France makes cars, cloth, aircraft, machines and **electrical goods**. **Tourism** is also very important.

Words you can learn

bonjour (bon-jewer)	hello
au revoir (oh-rev-wa)	goodbye
oui (we)	yes
non (noh)	no
merci (ma-r-see)	thank you
S'il vous plaît (cil voo play)	please
un (urn)	one
deux (de)	two
trois (twa)	three

Glossary

barge	a boat with a flat bottom. It can float in shallow water.
bonnet	a kind of hat that women wear
canal	a river dug by people
capital	the city where the government is based
dialect	the language spoken by people in one area
electrical goods	things like televisions and videos which use electricity
fashion	the way clothes look and what colour they are
harvest	the time when fruit, vegetables and corn are ready for the farmer to pick
meadow	grassy land
motorway	a big, fast road. Often they have three lanes of cars going each way.
parade	special carnival in the street
pétanque	a game like bowls
region	a part of a country
shutters	wooden flaps on each side of a window. They can be closed to keep the light out.
tourism	everything to do with visiting a place on holiday
wheat	plant used to make flour

Index